AUDIO
OBSCURA

AUDIO
OBSCURA

LAVINIA GREENLAW

PHOTOGRAPHS BY
JULIAN ABRAMS

Artangel
FULL CIRCLE EDITIONS

MANCHESTER
INTERNATIONAL
FESTIVAL

Introduction: Dark Listening

At a railway station, everyday dramas are constantly being played out: meeting, parting, anticipating, escaping. The atmosphere is an odd mix of tension and contemplation. Everyone is waiting for something to happen or moving between events. They might be there for minutes or hours, every day or just this one time. They are often silent, even those in couples and groups, and their thoughts are more than usually elsewhere. Many will be preoccupied by a displaced kind of talking or listening in the form of music or the mobile phone.

In a station, we are forced into proximity. We observe one another yet behave as if being in a crowd confers invisibility. We tend to assume that we are neither overheard nor overlooked.

The intimacy of a phone conversation overpowers the reality of the crowd. Moving through a crowd chatting to a friend does the same. Listening to music can absorb us to the point that we are unguarded about what our face, or body, might express.

Most of us don't set out to scrutinise those around us or to listen to their conversations yet we find that faces, gestures and phrases stand out and are remembered, whether we like it or not. Things catch our attention because they raise a question and fail to answer it. We are left in suspense. Why is that child crying or that woman laughing? What did he mean? Why are that couple not speaking? Who is he kissing? Why is she wearing that hat?

This book stands alone but derives from a sound work, also called Audio Obscura. Commissioned by Artangel and Manchester International Festival, it was created for Manchester Piccadilly and St. Pancras International stations, where these photographs were taken.

The idea comes from the camera obscura, or 'dark room', a once popular form of entertainment and artist's tool which uses a small aperture and mirrors to project a reflection of the passing world. A form of proto-cinema, the camera obscura was in part what led to early photography as people strove to fix the images it produced.

The framed and heightened image of the real has become how we receive the world (and even other worlds). We pay little attention to its construction and even less to the ways in which we construct it for ourselves. Jonathan Crary[1] has pointed out that 'some of the most pervasive means of producing "realistic" effects in mass visual culture, such as the stereoscope, were in fact based on a radical abstraction and reconstruction of optical experience.' This is also how memory operates; how we process what we fix. Audio Obscura is trying to achieve something similar. The texts are both fragment and essence, and the relation between each and its image is intended to sensitise us to an act that is so 'natural' that we often don't register it: the connections we impose on what we hear and what we see.

The fragile, shifting but acute images of the camera obscura draw you in. In Audio Obscura, the idea is translated into 'dark listening' with its connotations of depths and shadows, the impalpable and the unreachable. We enter interior lives and discover, somewhere between what is heard and what is seen, what cannot be said. We are conscious of this as transgression but unable to contain our curiosity. And we in turn become less self-aware: caught up in the act of listening, we give ourselves away.

Audio Obscura is situated in tension with our compulsion to construct narratives, to impose meaning, and to seek symmetry and conclusion. The texts hover between speech and thought. They are concentrated fragments of interior worlds which sensitise us to boundaries we depend upon yet break. They are drawn from the twelve monologues that form the basis of the sound work and they glance off one another, meet and diverge as a bigger picture coheres and dissolves like the reflections inside the camera obscura.

These are fragments of stories from which we might draw a whole story, as if extracting DNA. Making the sound work I focused on listening and found that what stayed in the mind, or contained the narrative, was often not the vivid concrete detail that we are told make stories memorable. It was the small words. The monologues were performed by actors and I edited them down from those recordings, not from the page. Each edit was tested in the context of a station, as a form of the overheard, and somehow these small words brought with them the force of the greater drama that had held them in place. Had I written them straight off, they would have seemed banal but excised from a voice, they had quite a different effect. They needed a context from which to be removed.

Sometimes the words are not small but over two years of listening I have taken away as many of them as possible. Whether a brief agitation or a slow realisation, however perturbing or insistent, what is heard should be as weightless as it can be – like thought. This editing process was done in collaboration with the sound designer Tim Barker, and together we learnt to listen to ourselves and to trust our visceral response. We also learnt how to stay in the dark. These stories are neither revealed nor concluded. The experience is not one of being told something but of becoming conscious of what we do with what we listen to. In this book, the listening occurs in the space between text and image when what is said meets what is seen.

All of my work has, in one form or another, been an exploration of the point at which we start to make sense of things; an attempt to arrest and investigate that moment, to separate its components and test their effects. Audio Obscura extends this to the act of listening, or dark listening, in which unconscious aspects of perception are brought to light in ourselves.

LG, April 2011

[1] *Techniques of the Observer: on vision and modernity in the 19th century,* Jonathan Crary, MIT Press 1992

All I needed to say ... it's all I needed to say.

That's exactly what I said, 'Most people.'

I've got everything on the list and I'm going to start tonight.

The thing is I don't feel anything.

Sometimes I want to go back.

All I ever dreamt of.

It doesn't look right. I can see that now.

I'm different because of it.

He wouldn't know about that. No one does.

No harm in it.

Socks. Water rates. Nail scissors. DNA.

Swimming things. Someone must have seen.

Bulbs for the garden. Oh god the garden.

When am I going to get round to the garden?

The pattern of cuts. Precise. Considered.

Right round her waist. What does that mean?

Round her waist. Like a belt only more delicate.

A chain. Almost a daisy chain. Such a tiny waist.

Affidavit. Lunch money. Wool.

They made her dance. Broken glass.

It'll happen again.

Lilies, for god's sake.

I went in the other day.

Just passing.

It was a work meeting.

In the middle of the working day.

We talked about work.

Every day it's as if they've never
seen each other before.
Never danced.

I want to say goodbye. Goodbye to someone and hello to someone. Hello and goodbye and let me know and have a good trip and see you soon and I'll miss you and don't forget and give us a kiss and don't forget and let me know and it's been lovely and come back soon.

When I said I couldn't hear them crying, well that wasn't true.

I knew they were crying.

I told him. All of it. How it wakes me up in the night—two or three times usually— and he didn't turn away or anything, just held my hand and said 'I'm here now.' And so I told him how long it takes and what it does and about all the mess and he just kept saying 'I'm not going anywhere. I'm here now.' And he is, isn't he?

They'll find out and they'll think I knew. But that's not what I saw. Not really. I only saw a list. You have to be absolutely sure. Or you've destroyed everything for nothing. Nothing. A list.

The big noise isn't stopping.

Someone please make it stop.

There are others.

What happened?

Was it my fault?

Let me come back.

Can you show me how to get back?

From a considerable height
and by some miracle, nothing broken.

I want you to know that someone has seen.

The shirt she tore.

The tie she didn't like.

The receipts.

I thought if the door was open, it would be alright to go in.

No need to knock or anything.

When she came back for her stuff
she couldn't even look me in the eye.
She didn't care and she wasn't sad.
She was excited.

They gather.

The same secrets, the same pain.

Then it's time and they're gone.

And more come.

Will I miss it?

I'll miss her.

I miss him.

I've missed it.

There's no one. No one to say he was always whatever and we loved how he did this and that and there was this time when we all and I will never forget how he and we never thought not for a minute that he'd be gone so soon and how we miss him we miss him so much and nothing will ever be the same without him and we will never stop loving and remembering and let us gather and let us pray.

Poor bird, I do not envy thee.

The first thing that struck me was the dark.

The kind that pushes itself into your eyes and mouth.

And the noise. Inside the mountain.

The hall of the mountain kings.

Ringing goblets. Clashing swords.

The echoing song and the whispering princess.

When they brought me out, I knew not to say.

Jagged mountains.

There's a tiny slippery crooked path.

The only way over and back down.

Swamps. Quicksand. Forests of briar.

Bubbling pools and fields of ice.

You should never say.

She's waiting.

Their faces.

She's been waiting for years.

Next Train To: Time Exptd Plat Train Destination Additional Information

Next Train To:	Time	Exptd	Plat	Train Destination	Additional Information
New Mills Cent	1403		4	New Mills Cent	Northern
New Mills Newt	1352		10	Buxton	Northern
Newport	1430		8	Milford Haven	Arriva Trains Wales
Newton Abbot	1407		6	Paignton	CrossCountry
Newton For Hyd	1418		3	Hadfield	Northern
Newton-le-will	1401		14	Liverpool L St	Northern
Northallerton	1357		3	Middlesbrough	TransPennine Express
Northwich	1417		11	Chester	Northern
Norwich	1343		13	Norwich	East Midlands Trains
Nottingham	1343		13	Norwich	East Midlands Trains
Oxenholme	1418		14	Edinburgh	TransPennine Express
Oxford	1427		8	Bournemouth	CrossCountry
Paignton	1407		6	Paignton	CrossCountry
Parbold	1422		14	Southport	Northern
Pembry & By Po	1430		8	Milford Haven	Arriva Trains Wales
Penrith	1418		14	Edinburgh	TransPennine Express
Peterborough	1343		13	Norwich	East Midlands Trains
Plumley	1417		11	Chester	Northern
Port Talbot Pw	1430		8	Milford Haven	Arriva Trains Wales
Preston Lancs	1354		14	Preston Lancs	TransPennine Express
Preston Lancs	1418		14	Edinburgh	TransPennine Express
Pyle	1430		8	Milford Haven	Arriva Trains Wales
Reading	1427		8	Bournemouth	CrossCountry
Reddish North	1403		4	New Mills Cent	Northern

Next Train To:	Time	Exptd	Plat	Train Destination	Additional Information
Rowsley	1403		4	New Mills Cent	Northern
Rose Hill Marp	1423		4	Rose Hill Marp	Northern
Ryder Brow	1403		4	New Mills Cent	Northern
Salford Cresce	1354		14	Preston Lancs	Northern
Sandbach	1404		12	Crewe	Northern
Scarborough	1411		13	Scarborough	TransPennine Express
Scunthorpe	1420		6	Cleethorpes	TransPennine Express
Seamer	1411		13	Scarborough	TransPennine Express
Sheff Meadowha	1420		6	Cleethorpes	TransPennine Express
Sheffield	1343		13	Norwich	East Midlands Trains
Sheffield	1420		6	Cleethorpes	TransPennine Express
Shrewsbury	1430		8	Milford Haven	Arriva Trains Wales
Southampton Al	1427		9	Bournemouth	CrossCountry
Southampton C	1427		9	Bournemouth	CrossCountry
Southport	1422		14	Southport	Northern
St Helens Jn	1401		14	Liverpool L St	Northern
Stafford	1407		6	Paignton	CrossCountry
Stalybridge	1411		13	Scarborough	TransPennine Express
Stockport	1343		13	Norwich	East Midlands Trains
Stockport	1355		7	London Euston	Virgin Trains
Stockport	1407		6	Paignton	CrossCountry
Stockport	1420		6	Cleethorpes	TransPennine Express
Stockport	1430		8	Milford Haven	Arriva Trains Wales

6

7

8

A to Z destinations, departure times are displayed for approximately the next 30 minutes

A to Z destinations, departure times are displayed for approximately the next 30 minutes

Currently, cancelled trains are not displayed on this screen.

ℹ Information   ℹ Information   ℹ Information   ℹ Info

Train times

When they took me in and we didn't know what was what, I made a promise.

He looked so proud. I mustn't say.

Four years.

Best not to say.

Please take this anger and this pain

and let me feel the love I know I have

and let me be able to speak of love

and show love and let me walk free

and let it fall away, the terrible weight and the pain,

and let me be good as I am good in my heart

and let it not hurt to remember

and let it stop and let me leave behind

all that has built itself into my heart

and let me find the words

and let there be time and let me open my heart

and let the hope be met with love

and all the wanting be simple and good

and let me be loved

and let me be allowed to be good.

Footsteps. Tannoy. Ringtone. Cough. Wheels. Door. Whisper. Brakes. Laugh. Bell. Swish. Platform Five. Sniff. Ringtone. Tannoy. Footsteps. Coins. Water. Steam. Footsteps. Wheels. Shout. Ringtone. Platform Five. Barrier. Sigh. Wheels. Footsteps. Shout. Rustle. Step. Platform Five. Sniff. Click. Cough. Wheels. Barrier. Platform Five. Clatter. Wheels. Wheels. Step. Step. Step.

Published to coincide with
Lavinia Greenlaw's
AUDIO OBSCURA

Manchester, Piccadilly Station
2 – 17 July 2011

St. Pancras International, London
13 September – 23 October 2011

Audio Obscura commissioned
and produced by Artangel and
Manchester International Festival

Presented at Manchester Piccadilly and at
St. Pancras International with the generous
financial support of Emmanuel Roman and
the kind co-operation of Network Rail

Special thanks to:
Tim Barker, Harry Escott, Ingrid Hu,
Amy Hubbard CSA, Simon Cox, Ed de Lacy,
Somethin' Else

First published in 2011 by Full Circle Editions

Printed in the UK in an edition of 2,500 copies

Publication © Lavinia Greenlaw, Artangel and
Manchester International Festival, 2011
Photographs © Julian Abrams, 2011
The moral right of the author and artist has
been asserted.

Design and layout copyright © Full Circle
Editions 2011
Parham House Barn, Brick Lane,
Framlingham, Woodbridge, Suffolk IP13 9LQ

www.fullcircle–editions.co.uk

Set in Chronicle Deck
Paper: Arctic Volume White 130gsm from
FSC Mixed Sources

Book design: Jonathan Christie
Printed and bound in Suffolk by Healeys Print
Group, Ipswich.

ISBN 978-0-9561869-7-3

Artangel

Based in London but working across Britain and beyond, Artangel has forged an
international reputation commissioning and producing exceptional projects by
outstanding contemporary artists. Since 1991, these projects have materialised in
a range of different sites and situations and across all forms of media.

James Lingwood/Michael Morris: Co-Directors
Rachel Anderson: Head of Interaction
Alice Boff: Administrative Assistant
Rob Bowman: Head of Programmes and Production
Maria Carroll: Head of Development
Sarah Davies: Development and Publicity Coordinator
Seb Emina: Web Editor
Cressida Hubbard: Administrative Director
Gabrielle Lecocq: Finance Assistant
Sinéad McCarthy: Production Assistant
Ryan Murray: Interaction Associate
Eleanor Nairne: Collections Coordinator

www.artangel.org.uk

Artangel is generously funded by Arts Council England and the private
patronage of:

Artangel International Circle: Inge & Cees de Bruin, Andrea & Guy Dellal,
Marie & Joe Donnelly, Tania & Fares Fares, Wendy Fisher, Mala Gaonkar &
Oliver Haarmann, Samantha & John Hunt, Elizabeth Kabler, Jennifer
McSweeney, Han Nefkens, Catherine & Franck Petitgas, Gilberto Pozzi,
Pascale Revert & Peter Wheeler, Barrie & Emmanuel Roman, Cora & Kaveh
Sheibani, Manuela & Iwan Wirth, Anita & Poju Zabludowicz, Michael Zilkha

Special Angels: Meg Allen, Shane Akeroyd, Laura & William Burlington,
Julie & Fred Chauffier, Carolyn Dailey, Karen & Ferdinand Groos,
Harry Handelsman & Elizabeth Crompton-Batt, Maria de Madariaga &
Anthony Vanger, Fatima & Eskander Maleki, Brian McMahon, Gilberto Pozzi,
Kadee Robbins, Luisa & Marco Rossi, Dasha Shenkman, Helen Thorpe,
Geoff Westmore & Paula Clemett, Helen & Edward White

and The Company of Angels

Manchester International Festival

Manchester International Festival (MIF) is the world's first festival of original,
new work and special events. It takes place biennially in July in Manchester, UK.
It is an artist-led, commissioning festival working with leading artists from
around the world to present new work from across the spectrum of performing
arts, music, visual arts and popular culture. Many MIF commissions, having had
their world premiere in Manchester, then go on to tour the world.

Alex Poots: Festival Director
Simon Mellor: General Director
Christine Cort: Associate Director
Jackie McNerney: Administrative Director
Jack Thompson: Technical Director
Kerenza McClarnan: Producer

www.mif.co.uk